Making puppets

James Dunbar

This book tells you about five different sorts of puppets. It also tells you how to make them.

You do not have to read this book from beginning to end, but do follow the instructions carefully if you are making a puppet.

Contents

Finger puppets

You use your fingers to make a finger puppet.

When you move your fingers the puppet comes alive.

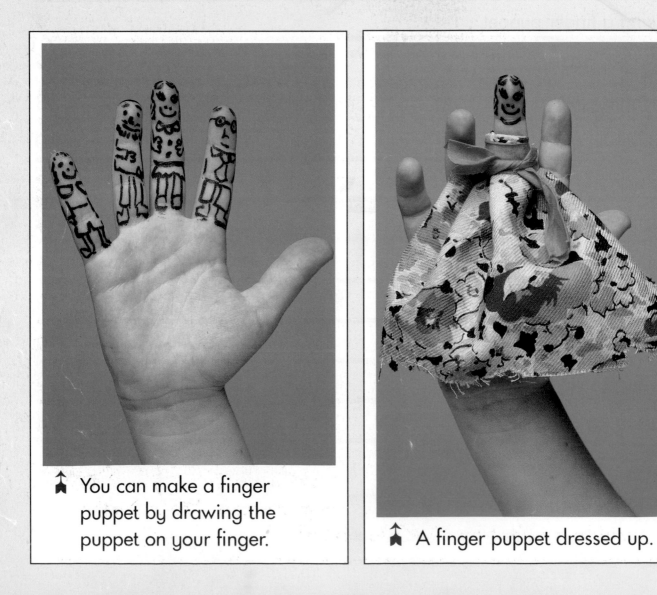

⬆ You can make a finger puppet by drawing the puppet on your finger.

⬆ A finger puppet dressed up.

Some finger puppets have heads.
The head fits on your finger.
You can use matchboxes or table tennis balls.

Two of these puppets are made from matchboxes. The one in the middle is made from a table tennis ball.

Making a finger puppet

Your fingers are the legs for this puppet.

You will need:
a piece of cardboard
scissors
crayons

1. Draw the outline of this puppet onto cardboard.
2. Then cut the puppet out.
3. Cut out the two circles for your fingers.
   You may need help with this.
4. Draw a person onto the cardboard.
5. Colour it in.

6. Fold the cardboard back on the dotted line.

7. Put your fingers through the holes.

Now the puppet can walk and dance.

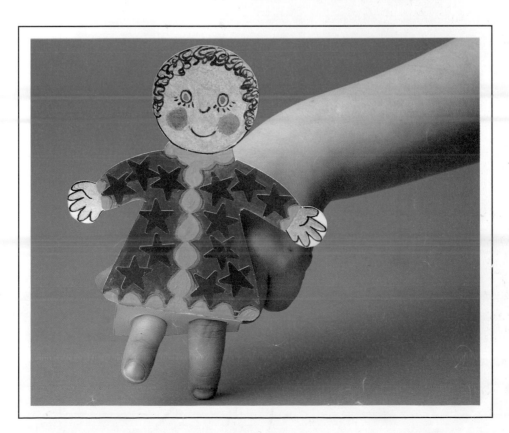

Glove puppets

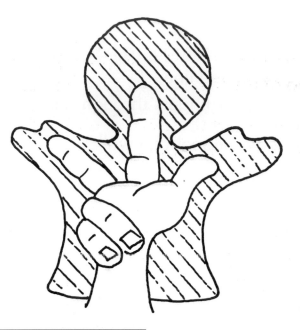

A glove puppet fits on your hand like a glove.

Your pointing finger fits into the puppet's head.

Your thumb and second finger are the puppet's arms.

⬆ Sooty the bear is a glove puppet.

There are many famous glove puppets.
Two of the the most famous are Punch and Judy.

The heads of these Punch and Judy puppets
are carved out of wood.

Making a glove puppet

First you make the head and neck.

You will need:
a tennis ball
an old sock
a piece of material 50 cm square
a piece of string 20 cm long
a rubber band
a cardboard tube
(or toilet roll)
scissors
pieces of wool
double-sided sticky tape or glue

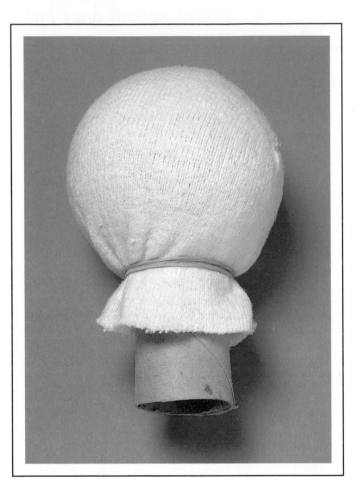

1. Find an old sock or stocking and a tennis ball.
2. Push the ball down into the toe part of the sock.
3. Cut the cardboard tube so it is a bit longer than your finger.
4. Put the tube down the sock until it is right up to the ball.
5. Attach the sock to the tube with a rubber band. You may need some help with this.
6. Then cut the sock a bit shorter than the tube.

7. Paint the puppet's face onto the sock.

8. Stick some wool on the head for hair.
Use double-sided sticky tape or glue.

Adding the glove

1. Choose some cloth about 50 cm square.
2. Cut out two pieces of the material to the shape shown in the picture. They must be bigger than your hand.
3. Staple or sew the two pieces together.
4. Leave a hole at the top for the neck of the puppet. Leave another hole at the bottom for your hand.
5. Put the neck of the puppet into the hole left for it in the top of the glove.
6. Tie the two parts together tightly with the piece of string.

Rod puppets

Rod puppets are held in your hands.
The rods move the puppet.

One long rod works the puppet's body.
Other rods can be used to work the arms.

Making a rod puppet

You will need:
a block of foam rubber about 25 cm long,
15 cm wide and 10 cm thick
two pieces of string, each one 25 cm long
bits of foam rubber, for hair, eyes and nose
cloth, about 40 cm long and 60 cm wide
a wooden rod or cane about 50 cm long
scissors
paints
double-sided sticky tape or glue

1. Tie one piece of string tightly around the block of foam rubber, about 7 cm from the bottom. This makes the head, neck and shoulders.
2. Use scissors to cut the head to the shape you want.
3. Poke a hole in the base of the puppet with scissors.
   You may need some help with this.
4. Push the rod about 10 cm into the hole.

14

5. Cut the shapes for the nose, eyes, ears and hair out of the bits of foam rubber.

6. Stick the pieces onto the head with double-sided sticky tape or glue. Paint in the eyes, nose and mouth. Wrap the cloth around the puppet's neck like a cloak and tie it tightly with the other piece of string.

Now the puppet is ready.

Shadow puppets

You can make shadows act like puppets.

You can make shadows with your hands.
You can make them look like animals.
Shadow puppets work in the same way.

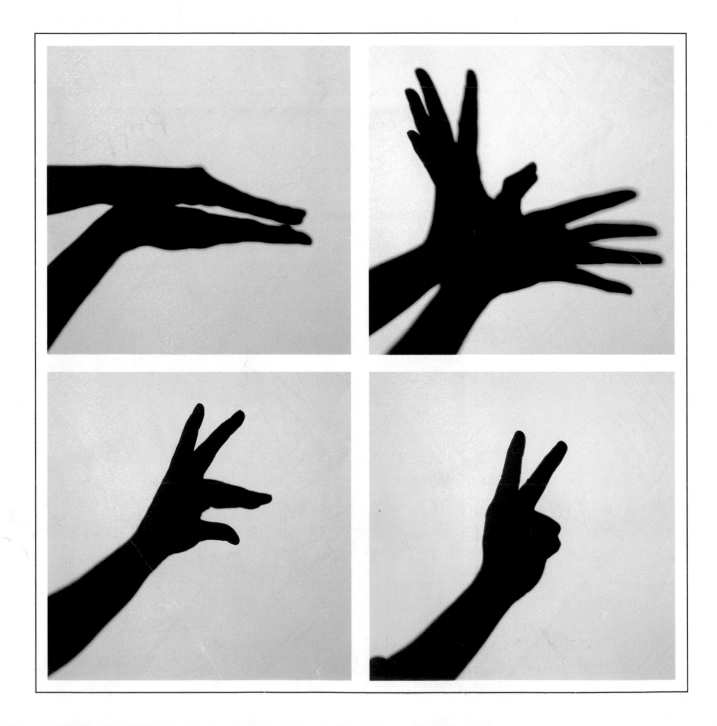

It is the patterns and holes on the puppet that make the
shape of the shadow so interesting.

⬆ An old shadow puppet from a country called Java.
The hands are controlled with rods.

Making a dragon shadow puppet

You will need:

a wooden rod or cane, about 35 cm long

8 paper fasteners (butterfly clips)

2 lengths of strong wire, both about 30 cm long

scissors

paints

a roll of sticky tape

cardboard about 40 cm long and 30 cm wide

1. Copy the dragon shapes onto the cardboard.
2. Cut out the shapes.
3. Get a grown-up to make holes where the dots are.
4. Join the puppet together using the paper fasteners.
   Match up the numbers to get the right pieces together.
5. Paint your dragon.
6. Stick the rod to the back of the dragon's body
   (with the sticky tape).
7. Put a piece of wire through the dragon's chin.
   Bend the wire so it cannot come out.
8. Put a piece of wire through the dragon's tail. Bend the wire.
9. Put the puppet about 60 cm in front of a light shining on
   a wall and you will then see its shadow.

String puppets

You make string puppets move by pulling their strings.

The strings are tied to the head, arms and legs.
String puppets are also called marionettes.

The Indian dancer needs lots of strings but the mouse needs only three.

Making a string puppet

You will need:
a thin piece of wood or stick, 20 cm long
a reel of strong thread and a needle
a piece of string, 20 cm long
2 pieces of string, 35 cm long
a tennis ball
a piece of cloth about 50 cm square
paints

1. Spread out the cloth and put the ball in the middle.
2. Fold the cloth over the ball. Then wrap it tightly around the ball.
3. Tie the cloth tightly up to the ball. This is now the head and body.
4. Spread out the body of the puppet as it is shown in the picture.

5. Tie thread around the ends of the cloth to make the hands.
6. Paint the puppet.
7. Put the strings on the puppet. Follow the diagram carefully.

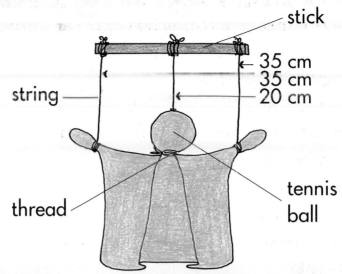

stick

35 cm
35 cm
20 cm

string

thread

tennis ball

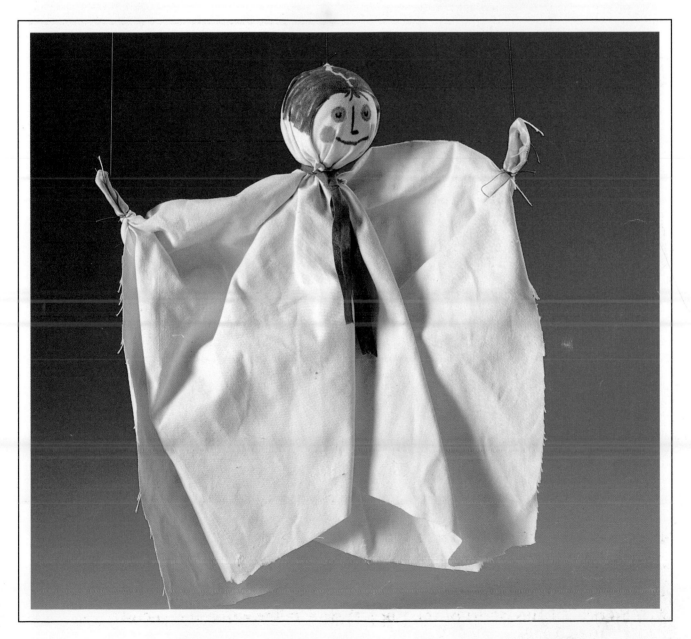

More string puppets

String puppets from the Little Angel Theatre in London.